FUNNY JOKES FOR 7 YEAR OLD KIDS

100+ Crazy Jokes That Will Make You Laugh Out Loud!

Cooper the Pooper

© Copyright 2021 Cooper the Pooper - All rights reserved.

The content contained within this book may not be reproduced, duplicated or transmitted without direct written permission from the author or the publisher.

Under no circumstances will any blame or legal responsibility be held against the publisher, or author, for any damages, reparation or monetary loss due to the information contained within this book, either directly or indirectly.

Legal Notice:

This book is copyright protected. It is only for personal use. You cannot amend, distribute, sell, use, quote or paraphrase any part, or the content within this book, without the consent of the author or publisher.

Disclaimer Notice:

Please note the information contained within this document is for educational and entertainment purposes only. All effort has been executed to present accurate, up to date, reliable, complete information. No warranties of any kind are declared or implied. Readers acknowledge that the author is not engaged in the rendering of legal, financial, medical or professional advice. The content within this book has been derived from various sources. Please consult a licensed professional before attempting any techniques outlined in this book.

By reading this document, the reader agrees that under no circumstances is the author responsible for any losses, direct or indirect, that are incurred as a result of the use of the information contained within this document, including, but not limited to, errors, omissions or inaccuracies.

TABLE OF CONTENTS

Table of Contents 3

Introduction 4

Chapter 1: Funny Jokes 6

Chapter 2: Crazy Jokes 18

Chapter 3: Laugh-out-Loud Jokes 30

Chapter 4: Knock-Knock Jokes 42

Chapter 5: Bonus Jokes 54

Final Words 66

INTRODUCTION

When I was a puppy, I loved telling jokes. I mean, coming up with ways to make people laugh — I could not think of anything better.

And just to be clear, I made a lot of people laugh.

Which is exactly the reason I decided to write this book.

See, in your hand you have what I believe to be my best piece of work. You are currently holding a book I wrote that is absolutely full to the brim with the fantastically hilarious jokes written just for seven-year-old kids.

But please know that these are not just any old jokes.

In fact, it has taken me years to put this book together. Over the last ten years I have traveled the world looking for the funniest jokes on the planet — and to be honest, I think I might have found every single one.

In between these pages you are going to find jokes about monsters, about animals, about food, and anything else you could possibly imagine. And as a result, you are going to laughing non-stop from start to finish.

And it gets even better.

Something I have learned over the last few years is that these jokes get better the more people you share them with. Which means you are going to have to remember your favorites so you can share them with your friends and family time and time again.

Just make sure you don't break a funny bone!

So, what are you waiting for? Turn the first page and start reading the funniest jokes for seven-year-old kids on the planet.

CHAPTER 1
FUNNY JOKES

1

What is blue but not heavy?

- **Light blue.**

2

What do you call a bee that's having a bad hair day?

- **A frisbee.**

3

What's a witch's favorite make-up?

- **Ma-scare-a!**

4

What do you call a witch with chickenpox?

- **An itchy witchy.**

5

My dad: You missed school yesterday!

- Me: To tell you the truth, I didn't really miss it.

6

How do skeletons tell their future?

- They look at their HORRORscope!

What kind of button won't unbutton?

- **A belly button.**

How do you cut a wave in half?

- **You use a sea-saw.**

9

What do you call a boy named Lee who no one talks to?

- Lonely.

10

Want to hear a roof joke?

- This first one's on the house.

How does a scientist freshen her breath?

- **With experi-mints!**

Where do zombies go swimming?

- **The Dead Sea.**

13

What do you need to bring to music class?

- **A note-book.**

14

What do you get when you cross a teacher and a vampire?

- **Lots of blood tests.**

Why did the skeleton drink eight glasses of milk every day?

- **Milk is good for the bones.**

Why didn't the girl trust the ocean?

- **There was something fishy about it.**

What do you call a snowman's kids?

- **Chilled-ren.**

What did the banana say to the dog?

- **Nothing. Bananas can't talk.**

19

What's a cat's favorite magazine?

- A cat-alogue.

20

What kind of music do mummies love?

- Wrap music.

Are black cats bad luck?

- **Sure, if you're a mouse.**

Where do ghosts buy their food?

At the ghostery store.

1

Why did the broom get a poor grade in school?

- **Because it was always sweeping during class.**

2

Teacher: "Don't you know you can't sleep in my class?"

- **Student: "I know. But maybe if you were just a little quieter, I could."**

Why did the doctor install a knocker on his door?

- **He wanted to win the "no bell" prize.**

What are ghosts' favorite trees?

- **Ceme-trees.**

5

What did the beach say to the tide when it came in?

- Long time no sea.

6

What did one ice cube say to the other?

- "I'm cooler than you!"

What has keys but no doors, has space but no rooms, and you can enter but never leave?

- **A keyboard!**

What did one flame say to the other?

- **"We're a perfect match."**

9

What do you call a cow on a trampoline?

- **A milkshake!**

10

What do you call cheese that's not yours?

- **Na-cho Cheese!**

How do you know if there's an elephant under your bed?

- **Your head hits the ceiling!**

What do you call two birds in love?

- **Tweethearts.**

13

Why did the cookie go to the hospital?

- **Because he felt crummy.**

14

What did the limestone say to the geologist?

- **Don't take me for granite.**

What do you say to a rabbit on its birthday?

- **Hoppy Birthday.**

What happens when a vampire walks in the snow?

- **Frost bite.**

How do ghosts wash their hair?

- **With sham-boo.**

What did the cheerleader say to the ghost?

- **Show your spirit.**

19

What goes "tick-tock" and "woof-woof?"

- **A watchdog.**

20

Why do shoemakers go to heaven?

- **Because they have good soles.**

Why did the girl put her cake in the freezer?

- **She wanted to ice it.**

Does a green candle burn longer than a pink one?

- **No, they both burn shorter.**

CHAPTER 3
LAUGH-OUT-LOUD JOKES

1

What did one tube of glue say to the other?

- **"Let's stick together."**

2

What does a rain cloud wear under her dress?

- **Thunderwear!**

3

What's the difference between a guitar and a fish?

- You can tune a guitar, but you can't tuna fish.

4

How did the barber win the race?

- He knew a short cut.

5

How does a cucumber become a pickle?

- It goes through a jarring experience.

6

What did one toilet say to the other?

- You look a bit flushed.

Why was the math book sad?

- Because it had too many problems.

Why does nobody talk to circles?

- Because there's no point.

What do you give a sick bird?

- **Tweetment!**

What do you call two witches living together?

- **Broommates.**

11

What's big, scary and has three wheels?

- A monster on a tricycle.

12

What do you get when Santa becomes a detective?

- Santa clues.

13

Why did the kid bring a ladder to school?

- **Because she wanted to go to high school.**

14

What did the tiger say to her cub on his birthday?

- **It's roar birthday.**

What do you call guys who love math?

- **Algebros.**

How do you stay warm in any room?

- **Go to the corner — it's always 90 degrees.**

What kind of tree you can hold in your hand?

- **A palm tree!**

What do cats like to eat on a hot day?

- **A bowl of mice cream!**

19

What is worse than a dog howling at the moon?

• Two dogs howling at the moon.

20

How do you tell the difference between an elephant and a mouse?

• Try picking them up!

Why did the computer go to the dentist?

- It had a blue tooth.

What did one wall say to the other wall?

- I'll meet you at the corner!

Knock, knock!

Who's there?

Debra.

Debra who?

Debra Cadabra!

Knock, knock!

Who's there?

Don.

Don who?

Don ask silly questions!!

3

Knock, knock!

Who's there?
Mice.

Mice who?
No, owls do!

4

Knock, knock!

Who's there?
Eggs.

Eggs who?
Eggs-cuse me, you drove over my flowers.

5

Knock, knock!

Who's there?

Dawn.

Dawn who?

Dawn leave me out here in the cold!

6

Knock, knock!

Who's there?

Al.

Al who?

Al be seeing you later.

7

Knock, Knock!

Who's there?

Russia.

Russia who?

Russia through your meal and you'll be sick!

8

Knock, Knock!

Who's there?

Sweden.

Sweden who?

Sweden sour chicken is my favorite!

9

Knock, knock!
Who's there?
Venice.

Venice who?
Venice your mother coming home?

10

Knock, knock!
Who's there?
Ant.

Ant who?
Antarctic!

Knock, knock!
Who's there?
Armenia.

Armenia who?
Armenia every word I say!

Knock, knock!
Who's there?
Ahmed.

Ahmed who?
Ahmed a mistake. Please give me an eraser.

13

Knock, knock!

Who's there?
Rita.

Rita who?
Rita book; you might learn something!

14

Knock, knock!

Who's there?
Ken.

Ken who?
Ken you let me in?

15

Knock, knock!

Who's there?

Andrew.

Andrew who?

Andrew a picture on the wall.

16

Knock, knock!

Who's there?

Annie.

Annie who?

Annie more of these knock-knock jokes?

Knock, knock!

Who's there?

Egg.

Egg who?

Eggcited to see me?

Knock, knock!

Who's there?

Abe.

Abe who?

Abe C D E F G...

Knock, knock!

Who's there?

Bored.

Bored who?

Bored of education!

Knock, knock!

Who's there?

Ears.

Ears who?

Ears some more knock-knock jokes for you!

21

Knock, Knock!
Who's there?
Elsie.
Elsie who?
Elsie you around!

22

Knock, Knock!
Who's there?
Philip.
Philip who?
Philip my glass, will you please?!

Why didn't the robot finish his breakfast?

- **Because the orange juice told him to concentrate.**

What is the strongest creature in the world?

- **The snail; it carries its whole house on its back.**

3

What position does Dracula like to play in baseball?

- **Bat!**

4

Why couldn't the bees catch the bus?

- **They missed the buzz stop.**

What has only one eye but still can't see?

- **A needle.**

What did the pencil say to the paper?

- **Write on!**

Why did the banana go to the doctor?

- It wasn't peeling well.

What has hands but can't clap?

- A clock!

9

What did the little tree say to the big tree?

- **Leaf me alone!**

10

What is Spiderman's favorite month?

- **Web-ruary!**

11

What's a math teacher's favorite season?

- Sum-mer!

12

Which month do trees dislike?

- Sep-timber!

13

What do you call a pig that knows karate?

- **A pork chop!**

14

Why was the picture sent to prison?

- **It was framed.**

15

Where do hamburgers go to dance?

• The meat-ball.

16

What did the calculator say to the math student?

• You can count on me.

What did the digital clock say to the grandfather clock?

- **Look! No hands!**

Why wouldn't they let the butterfly into the dance?

- **Because it was a moth-ball.**

19

What do frogs order when they go to a restaurant?

- **French flies.**

20

Who comes to a picnic but is never invited?

- **Ants.**

FINAL WORDS

Firstly, I want to give you a massive thank you for reading my book.

Writing this book was a huge effort. It took years of research, traveling the globe, looking for great jokes so I could write the final product — and nothing makes me happier than knowing that great kids like you are reading them.

But remember, there is still more to do.

See, even though you made it to the end of the book, things are only just getting started.

It is time to go back through and pick out your favorite jokes so that you can share them with your friends and family — after all, the only thing better than hearing a funny joke is telling a funny joke.

So, what in the world are you waiting for — head back to the start of this book and prepare to share some laughs with everyone you know!

www.ingramcontent.com/pod-product-compliance
Lightning Source LLC
Chambersburg PA
CBHW071408070526
44578CB00002B/519